Take Me Out

Take Me Out

Bill Littlefield

ILLUSTRATIONS BY
Stephen Coren

ZEPHYR PRESS

Zephyr Press, a non-profit arts and education 501(c)(3) organization,
publishes literary titles that foster a deeper understanding of cultures
and languages. Zephyr Press books are distributed to the trade in the U.S.
and Canada by Consortium Book Sales and Distribution [www.cbsd.com]
and by Small Press Distribution [www.spdbooks.org].

Zephyr Press acknowledges with gratitude the financial support
of the Massachusetts Cultural Council.

massculturalcouncil.org

Cataloguing-in publication data is available from the Library of Congress.

ISBN 978-1-938890-09-3

ZEPHYR PRESS
50 Kenwood Street
Brookline, MA 02446

www.zephyrpress.org

Table of Contents

PUBLISHER'S COIN TOSS

Poems are games.

Not that poems are *like* games, or that they are metaphorically games. Poems are actual games. We mark out a defined arbitrary space, we follow or invent arbitrary rules, and that's what makes a game a game — whether we call it chess or a sonnet, stickball or *vers libre*, hockey or haiku.

We all know people who take games — including the great variety of poetry games — far too seriously. And occasionally a game transcends its own field of play to ring with a more universal resonance. But there are damned few of these. We need to cherish, as this book does, those for whom a game is something you *play*.

Bill Littlefield, first and foremost a writer, plays games even as he writes about them. He unabashedly versifies not for profit, cosmic meaning, or a championship cup, but for fun. He makes no bones about it: these verses are doggerel, defined in the OED as "comic or burlesque verse, usually of irregular rhythm . . . mean, trivial, or undignified verse." And while there is nothing mean or trivial in the lines that follow here, much is exuberantly undignified. The rhythms, too, are sharper than they might look at first glance — Read them aloud. Doggerel rhythms and rhymes have an honorable place in grown-up English letters, at least since Chaucer's day, both unself-consciously, as in the touching and ludicrous verse of William McGonagall; or self-consciously, as in the urbane lyrics of Ogden Nash. And radio, which has long been Littlefield's primary medium, proves an encouraging breeding-ground for light verse of various kinds.

Littlefield himself originally thought of these poems as amusement for children; but, while we confidently expect children to delight in them, we offer them for adults, the most accomplished players and appreciative followers of sports and games. Committed to publishing books that serve as bridges between cultures, Zephyr can assert that *Take Me Out* spans the gap between those sometimes alien civilizations of childhood and adulthood.

GAME DAY

You wake up almost singing at the promise of the day.
You know before you really know it that you're gonna play.
Your uniform is draped across the bedroom's only chair,
And you are not surprised. Hey! it was you who put it there.
(You had to when your Mom said, "No! You can't wear that to bed!")
You did the next best thing and hung it on the chair instead.
You hardly taste your breakfast. You're already at the court,
Or at the rink, or on the field, and wondering what sort
Of day you're gonna have when someone's handed you the ball,
Or dropped the puck, or blown the whistle. Happily it's all
The same when you're a player, and the day before you seems
To be there as a promise and the answer to your dreams.

PLANE VIEW

A football field looks peaceful when you see it from a plane.
That's even when a game is on, and even in the rain.
The lines suggest an order that's impossible to see
Unless you're miles above the ground, as you are bound to be
If you are in an airplane, in the day or in the dark,
If you should chance to look down on a peaceful football park.

I've also noticed swimming pools when I've been flying by,
As they have sparkled far below my seat up in the sky.
It seems to me they're always empty, all those swimming pools,
As if no one could swim without ignoring someone's rules.

I've also gazed at tennis clubs when I've peered down at sports.
There's nothing quite as orderly as lots of tennis courts
Set side by side in several rows as if some giant hand
Had placed a ruler carefully across that bit of land
And drawn along the ruler's sides straight edges to define
Where "in" would be, and also "out" according to the line.

And then, of course, the diamonds shining brightly far below
Declare themselves as places where the baseball games should go,
Although from many thousand feet I couldn't really tell,
If anyone among those players might be playing well.

Up high above the fields and courts and diamonds, there's no sound.
The players, should they look up, would not know where I am bound.
That is, if there are players on those tidy yards below.
From where I sit above them, it is difficult to know.

THE VOCABULARY OF SPORTS

Forehand, backhand, drop shot, dunk,
Lay-up, slap shot, fastball, skunk —
Wait! There are no skunks in sports —
Curveball, crawl stroke, fame reports,
Backhand, topspin, serve and volley,
"Screwball" is a term that's jolly.

Backboard, backstop, backspin, putt,
Dog leg, sand trap, duck hook, what?
Whiff, three-bagger, dinger, fade,
Slice, free kick, and lemonade.
What has lemonade to do
With sports? You ask, and though it's true
I cannot give an answer back,
I know it's good with any snack.

(If all these words have got you thinking
Of what *you'd* like to be drinking,
Lemonade might hit the spot.
I know I like it quite a lot.)

Meanwhile, pitch out, pump fake, steal.
You needn't, if you see one, squeal,
For stealing bases is okay —

The red zone, passed ball, double play.
A heave's a throw. A throw's a peg,
And cricket has left silly leg.
I could go on, and so could you.
There is no doubt: I'm sure it's true.

I think this game has been well played.
We've *earned*, perhaps, that lemonade.

IMAGINING A GAME

For some games you must have a field. For some you need a court.
For lots of them you need a ball, or new shoes of some sort.
For some you need a racket, and perhaps a helmet, too.
And lots of games require lots of people, not just you.

If you don't have the things you need — the field, the court, the shoes,
You might find that you have those awful *I don't have that* blues.
But don't let all that get you down. Don't worry, fret, or weep,
For you can do — while wide awake — what we all do in sleep.
Just dream yourself a stadium and fans to fill it, too,
A great big park with lots of folks who've come to cheer for you.
Then step up to the plate you've thought up, as your dream takes wing,
And when the pitch comes in, think up the perfect home-run swing.
It won't be long, I'm sure, before you're playing games for real.
But try just making up a game to see how it will feel.

THEY MIGHT NOT BE GIANTS

Olympians need not be giants.
They need not be tall.
The female gymnasts at the Games
Are sometimes kind of small.

"BEST OF" SHOW

Let us now praise famous men
Before they praise themselves again:

The pitchers making millions, who,
Could not retire me or you;

The goalie, nimble as a brick,
Who's slow and thoughtful — never quick;

The golfer who, inclined to flub
A shot then tosses his golf club

Into the air, through which it sails . . .
With luck there's no one it impales.

Oh, sing a song of those who ride
Their cycles uphill, side by side,

And hope that when the day is done
And they have had their riding fun

They won't be found the next day moping,
Since they have been pinched for doping.

Oh, hip hooray for college stars
Who while away their time in bars

Until the ending of the night
When it is time to start a fight,

And since a fight is not much fun
Unless somebody has a gun,

Pull out the heat and let 'er rip
And kiss goodbye that scholarship.

We can't forget the coaches who,
To win will do what they must do —

If that includes a transcript change
It's no big deal to rearrange

An "F" until, just like a tree,
It grows, and turns into a "B."

And let us not leave out the owners:
Greedy sots, eternal moaners,

Claiming they are losing money —
T'weren't so sad, it would be funny . . .

Give them buildings new and pretty,
Or they'll find another city

Where they will set up their teams
As someone else's nightly dreams.

My, our games must be fantastic,
Or our standards quite elastic

To endure the stupid stuff,
Some disgusting, some just fluff,

That's built around the brief, bright time
When what we're given is sublime.

ON APPRECIATION

Hooray for those who run and jump.
Hooray for those who score.
I watch, and they astonish me,
And who could ask for more?

Hooray for those who hit and pitch,
And those who catch the ball . . .
I wonder at their talents and
I'm dazzled by them all.

The best among them comes in first,
And lifts to us his cap.
I'm worn out merely watching him.
I think I'll take a nap.

ON BEING A FAN

Perhaps you are a Tigers fan.
You go to see them when you can,
And wear, perhaps, some tiger stripes.
But fans occur in different types
And different sorts
In different sports
And so the games go on.

Perhaps you choose to back a team
That rarely wins. Still, you can dream
Of some bright day
Calloo, callay!
When they will wear the victor's crown
And ride in a parade downtown.

Perhaps you back the Pirates! Yar!
For pirates, whether near or far
Or in the present or the past
Say "Yar!" a lot, and then "Avast!"
And "Matey!" They say "Matey," too.
At least I'm told that Pirates do.
The Mighty Ducks, a hockey team,
Have led their loyal fans to dream

Of Stanley Cups set end to end,
But I can tell you now, my friend,
That you will have a good long wait
Before a duck will learn to skate,
Although perhaps it's no more dumb
Than Tigers hitting baseballs. Some
Might say that Bears in football cleats
Would look quite silly. No one meets
A Dolphin in a helmet, no,
Nor did a Penguin ever go
A-whacking with a hockey stick,
And it would be a nifty trick
If Lions, when they heard the call,
Went chasing after a loose ball
Late fumbled by an Eagle or
A Falcon trying hard to score.
I guess we can't expect to claim
There's sense in each and every name
That every team has on its shirts,
But I am thrilled that mites and squirts
And midgets and some tadpoles, too,
Can play in games with folks like you.

THE NATURAL

Once I knew a boy who played a dozen different sports.
He played them all so well, according to the news reports,
That coaches at a hundred schools would call him up each day
And beg him to sign up with them so he could come and play.

(They knew he'd help their teams to win. The promised him great fame,
And said that everywhere the crowds would loudly shout his name.)

The boy would listen quietly to what the coaches said.
But by their happy promises he wouldn't be misled.
For them, he was an athlete first, but he was less than sure
That sports was something in his life as likely to endure
As learning how to tackle problems off the football field.
Perhaps he'd be a doctor or a teacher and not yield
To those who thought he ought to grab the glory that was there
For athletes who could learn to love the spotlight's blinding glare.
He puzzled all the coaches. He confused his friends as well,
And why he chose to walk away from glory, who can tell?
But I have heard he's happy with the choices he has made,
Which doesn't mean he didn't like the games that he had played.
It's just that he saw games as games, and *only* games, it seems,
And games took second place to all his more important dreams.

TO BE A BALL

If I were bound to be a ball and was supposed to like it,
I wouldn't be a volleyball, for sometimes people spike it.

A golf ball, though it's shiny white, gets hammered with a club.
Perhaps you think that might be fun, but I don't think so, Bub.
Besides, although a golf ball gets to fly and then to roll,
It always seems to end up at the bottom of a hole.

Some tap a soccer ball or head it, others kick it — hard.
It travels quite a bit around a green and grassy yard,
But all that kicking? Don't you think it's sometimes bound to hurt?
And not all soccer fields are grass. Sometimes they're only dirt.

A football? Maybe, but just how does anyone stay humble
If everybody wants him on a play when there's a fumble?
And footballs do get kicked, of course, and maybe worse than that
Is when they hit the cross bar with a sharp, resounding "splat!"

So I would be a baseball, and a special baseball, too:
the one that broke a home-run record. Here's what I would do:
I'd sail into the hands of a collector of such things
As uniforms and bats and balls and old World Series rings,

And he or she would take me home, aware that I was grand,
And put me underneath a dome atop a wooden stand,
And folks would come to gawk and stare, and I would be a star,
And I would be retired, as the lucky balls all are.

FAIR PLAY

I'll watch the ballgame if the center fielder mows my lawn,
And if the shortstop feeds my daughter's mouse while we are gone,
And maybe, if the bullpen guys have time enough to do it,
They'll wash the picture window so that then we can see through it.

I'll care about the draft the NBA's about to run
If two or three tall guys can clean our gutters. When they're done,
They might wash off the ceiling in the shower. What the heck?
Each time I do it, man, I wake up with the stiffest neck
I've ever had since last I did the job, and who needs those?
Meanwhile, I'll go see hockey if the whistle ever blows,
When several Rangers and a Maple Leaf or L. A. King
Come over with a tamper and a cold pack. Here's the thing:
My driveway's got these holes. They're getting bigger all the time.
A wheel goes in, I might not get back out, so where's the crime
In asking if some hockey players might put in some patches?
And, while they're on the job, there are some small but ugly scratches
Across the Camry's door. A little touch-up paint, we're good.

Now, you may feel I'm out of bounds, and that I never should
Expect more from the players than their big contracts provide:
Exciting entertainment and a great, unscripted ride
From starting pitch to final out or long, last-second shot,
And most times I agree that's all there is and they are not
Obliged to earn my loyalty by any other means,

But lately life's been crowding in, so if the sticky screens
That likely need replacing could be dealt with by an end
Or quarterback or safety, then those guys would have a friend
In me. I'd buy a ticket, paint my face, and scream and cheer.
But otherwise, with all the chores I've got, I can't go near
A stadium or even a TV when games are going.
In fact, at times when normally the tube would be a-glowing
With baseball or with basketball or football or such stuff,
I might be doing laundry, which is not exactly tough —
A tennis pro could do it, or a golfer, it's a cinch.
The guys who drive in NASCAR all could manage in a pinch.
I know the athletes are supposed to have me all inspired,
But, heck, sometimes by Saturday, these jobs have got me tired,
And, though the athlete's mission is to bear my childlike dreams,
Right now I'd take some less dramatic "bearing." If that seems
Irrational and silly, well, I've no time to debate.
I said I'd pick the kids up, and I think I'm running late.

AN OWNER OWNS

An owner owns. He might own stones
That glitter, shine, and gleam.
He might own something else instead,
Perhaps a baseball team.

An owner makes a few mistakes,
His team slips from its groove.
Don't be surprised should he decide
His team would like to move.

The owner turns his pockets out.
"They're empty," he complains.
He speaks to you as if he's sure
You don't have any brains.

He tells you his expenses,
Quite enormous, always mount,
And he assumes that no one
In the audience can count.

"I need a stadium," he says.
"A new one full of seats
Where wealthy friends of mine can sit
Enjoying wealthy treats.

"I also need more parking
And a new road over there
For people in the brand new seats
So they won't have to care

"If traffic holds the peasants up
As blaring horns are beeping.
The wealthy, on their private road,
Must get home quick for sleeping."

The mayor nods like a dummy set
Upon the owner's knee,
And talks of what a blessing those new
Seats and roads will be.

"The city will be saved," he says,
"the owner should be praised."
The people stand and wonder if he's
Crooked, dumb or dazed.

The owners own. Taxpayers groan,
And schools and roads lose out.
It will be always thus until
The people raise a shout,
And tell the moaning owner,
"Hey, you want to go? Get out."

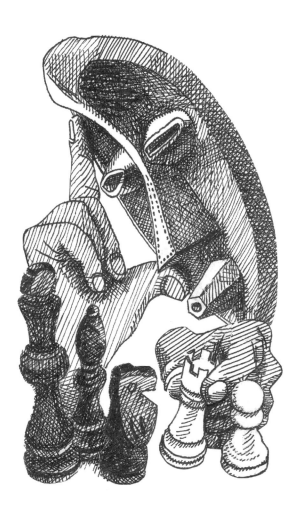

ZIPPY CHIPPY: A HORSE COMPLETE

Zippy Chippy wasn't zippy, for — despite his name —
He tended not to run a lot, although he wasn't lame.
One hundred times he entered races. Never did he win.
And sometimes Zippy just stood still, not choosing to begin.
The call would be "They're off!" But Zippy wasn't off at all.
He'd look around as if to say, "Let's go back to the stall."

Why, when other horses ran, would Zippy choose to be
The only one unmoved by dreams of mighty victory?
Some said that Zippy had no heart, and some said he was nuts.
One theory had it that he was a fumble-footed klutz.
But what if Zippy Chippy had a bigger brain than most?
And what if he knew winning was an empty sort of boast
If all the winning did was help some wealthy guy make money?
And what if Zippy found that idea sort of sad and funny?
And what if Zippy thought, "They're gonna feed me anyway.
Why work as if without the work I wouldn't get the hay?"

Zippy Chippy lives today upon a lovely farm.
And there he doesn't do a single living creature harm.
The people come to visit him and some of them conclude
That Zippy Chippy is a joke, and I would find that rude,
If I could not imagine somehow Zippy's worked it out:

Perhaps he chose to beat the game, then beat it in a rout.
He did not suffer injuries. He didn't suffer fools.
He got himself tossed off the track because of racing's rules,
Which say a horse that doesn't try cannot participate.
If Zippy figured that one out, I think it would be great.
For Zippy need not run these days, and still he gets to eat.
He lacks for neither food nor love. He is a horse complete.

RACING DAYS

In winter, working's easy. I just sit here at my screen
And type in what needs typing. Ah, you know the stuff I mean.
It might be hard to get to work, the driving might be tough,
But once I'm here, it's warm and bright, and that's about enough
To banish the distractions that might otherwise intrude
Upon the work of scribbling about our games, imbued
With concentration that's sufficient. Outside is a mess —
The cars slide into snow banks on the street below, so guess
Where I would rather be? Stuck in the weather or right here,
Just typing what needs typing? You can see, the choice is clear.

But come the month of August, working's quite another thing,
For, as I type, I know a little west of here the king
Of sports — or sport of kings — whichever — is transpiring daily
At Saratoga. Horses run, and all of them would pay me
If only I were there instead of here. I'm sure it's true.
I'd breakfast on fresh strawberries, and that's not all I'd do.
I'd sip hot coffee at the rail and figure all the races.
I'd pick not only winners, but the shows as well, and places.
But first I'd watch the morning works, and read and mark the form,
And marvel at the lawns of green, the air cleared by the storm
That washed away the heat that sometimes burdens trackside days.

They would be cool, those mornings, were I there, and all the bays
And blacks and chestnuts, grays as well, they'd see me standing there
And wink, and I would never miss the signals, and with care
But joyfully, I'd place my bets, and, when the day was done,
I'd wander into town and celebrate with what I'd won —
But celebrate with class and moderation, since the knack
Of picking winners means I'd have my breakfast at the track.
While losers still were sleeping, I would learn what losers missed,
Because they hadn't seen the horses pound out of the mist
Before the sun dispersed it and the crowd filled up the space . . .
I'd find myself in tune with that sweet track, that magic place.

Or so I like to think. It is the vision that I choose.
And if I don't attend the races, well — I never lose.

SWIMMING

There's swimming in the ocean, where the fish are sometimes scary,
And once, in a polluted lake, I saw one that looked hairy.

There's swimming in a river, where the fish are likely quick,
Unless the river's dirty. If it is, they might be sick.

And then there's swimming in a pool, which isn't so fantastic;
For though they're bright and colorful, the fish therein are plastic.

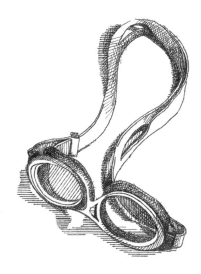

SWIMMING ... SORT OF

The ocean can be very cold. It's also very big.
A lake is sometimes sort of smelly, kind of like a pig:
Its bottom can be mucky, even yucky, slimy goo.
I wouldn't want to step in that and nor, I think, would you.

A river's fine to look at and it gurgles as it goes,
But where might rivers take me as they roll along? Who knows?
So never mind the ocean and the lakes and rivers, Bub.
My duck and I will only swim within our trusty tub.

RHYMING GOLF

Tennis rhymes with *menace*.
Can you find a rhyme for *darts*?
Hearts would seem too obvious.
A smelly answer? *F* * * * *

Basket-, *base-*, and *foot-* all share
the same last word: it's *ball*,
And *fall* rhymes well with that,
 and so do *call*, *wall*, *mall* and *Paul*.

Golf's a challenge as a game,
and where's a word that sounds
Like *golf*? I haven't found one,
although I've made the rounds

Of poets rhyming everywhere
and books of verses, too.
I guess I'll have to leave the task
of rhyming *golf* to you.

GOLF HERO

I sing today (or write, at least) of Mr. Tateyama,
A golfer in Japan whose name's a fine rhyme for pajama.
You won't have heard of him, I think, although he is a pro,
But Thursday he explored a realm that most will never know
No matter how much golf they play, how many shots they take.
Poor Mr. Tateyama made a terrible mistake
By setting out at all that day to try to play the game —
It may be that the world of golf will never be the same.

Upon the par-3 tee he stood. Who knows what he was thinking?
There is no evidence that in the clubhouse he'd been drinking,
But Mr. Tateyama launched his drive into the rough,
And hit his second shot astray, but that was not enough.
His third shot found some bushes far from the illusive green,
From there he whacked away until his tally was fourteen.

Yes, fourteen times did Mr. Tateyama swing his club
Against the fearsome bushes. Fourteen times the luckless schlub
Kept swinging. "I lost count," the tired golfer'd later say,
But others were still counting, and they counted all the way
To nineteen shots. That was the number Tateyama had
When he had finished up that par-3 hole. And was that bad?
Oh, that was not just bad, that nineteen was the worst, my friend.
It was the hole that Tateyama feared would never end.

And when it ended Tateyama held a record score,
For no pro in Japan had hit a golf ball any more
Than Tateyama had, which was remarkable, you see —
The hole was not par 5 or 4. That hole was a par 3.
So should we grieve for Tateyama? I don't think we should,
For out of his disaster there has come, I think, some good.

See, Mr. Tateyama never let it get him down —
I don't mean to suggest that he's a goofball or a clown,
But when the round was over, he could smile, and of the day
When on that par-3 hole he'd gone so thoroughly astray,
He said, "My mind went blank," and asked, "Have I a record now?"
Yes, Tateyama, yes, you do, And so, to you, I bow.

LIL

To make of athletes heroes often seems a little silly,
But if you're bound to do it, then consider Kristine Lilly.
No soccer-playing man has matched what Kristine Lilly's done.
She scored one hundred thirty goals and had sufficient fun
To carry her beyond the point where other players stop:
The list of most U. S. games played has "Lilly" at the top.
(And should you wonder at the number, as some people do,
The numeral in question is three hundred fifty-two.)

She won at the Olympics and she won at the World Cup.
And when the pro leagues faltered, well, she helped to prop them up.
She was and is and will be U. S. soccer's greatest light.
If you think *she's* a hero, then I'd have to say you're right.

CROQUET MADNESS

I went one day
To play croquet,
Believing it was quiet.

(A soccer game
Is not the same . . .
Sometimes there is a riot!)

But on this day
There was a fray
Upon the croquet pitch:

A mallet broke
Upon some bloke
Who'd called some lass a witch.

For she had clocked
The ball he'd knocked
Beside the final wicket,

And what was more,
As he did roar,
She told him where to stick it.

A TIME TO RUN

It's fun to run,
or so say some,
while others like to sit.

While I might walk
as I might talk,
I cheerfully admit

That what is fast
is in my past
as far as running goes,

For no one's knees
as stiff as these —
the ones above my toes —

Can ever bend
enough to send
a runner very far.

So run for fun
while you're still young,
if that is what you are.

WHAT RACERS DO

Racers race. That's what they do,
And they are fast, and noisy, too.
(Of quiet they are quite bereft,
Driving fast and turning left.)

Through headphones, as they speed along,
They hear instructions like a song
Screeching in the treble clef:
"Keep driving fast and turning left!"

Precisely where it had begun,
The race will end. It will be won,
For someone opposite of last
Kept turning left and driving fast.

LACROSSE

The Indians and Braves play baseball. Some would say, "Their loss."
Perhaps those some think Indians and Braves should play lacrosse.
Lacrosse, I'm told, was played upon the plains across land
Before the Indians and braves were made to understand
They had to leave the land they loved for regions quite forsaken:
The barren lots reserved for them, when better land was taken.

Lacrosse is played in high schools now and private schools as well.
It's played at lots of colleges, and I suppose that's swell.
Lacrosse requires running, passing, catching, shooting, too . . .
Though not the sort of shooting that the army liked to do
When Indians and braves would try remaining on their land,
As if perhaps when told to move they didn't understand.

A lot of people like lacrosse, which I suppose is nice.
To me it seems like slower hockey played without the ice.
But who am I to say what game is worst and which is best?
We each decide which one we think is better than the rest,
And if lacrosse is what you choose then I will understand,
And hope that in the days to come you never lose your land.

ROLLER DERBY

We went to watch the roller derby,
Me and Mom and her friend Herbie.
There we found the roaring sound
Of women going round and round
With elbows flying as they flew
Into each other, yes, it's true,
And tried to crash right through the pack
While circling round the roller track.

(I should say some of them were crashing,
Also churning, sometimes dashing,
Others just got in the way —
They have to do that when they play
At roller derby. It's their fate:
They also serve who block and wait . . .
Or so the blockers like to say.)
It's rough, but still they call it "play."

A funny thing about the sport
That I'm reluctant to report
Is that the women all are called
By names your granny'd be appalled

To hear, like Maya Mangleyou,
And Dottie Danger, yes, it's true,
And Belle Air Bomber, Lil' Paine,
And one they're calling Ms. Fright Train.

I wouldn't say that I'm a fan
Of those who roll because they can
Around the track as people cheer
Because to me it isn't clear
How points are scored or when they are,
Without a basket, goal or par.
They bump and crash and break away
And numbers pile up as they play
And somehow, later, as they do,
It's 3-0-6 to 2-5-2.

DERBY ROLLING

Nobody wears a derby any more.
No derby on the hat rack, no derby on the floor.

Time was you could see derbies here and there.
They covered heads a lot, and lots of hair.

Have derbies gone the way of blacksmith shops?
They don't seem much in evidence as tops
On men, who used to wear them everywhere.
Perhaps you think it's silly that I care.

Why do I? Why, the hat that I'm extolling
Is crucial for the sport of derby rolling.

WHACK IT

You whack it with a racquet that seems smallish for the job.
The ball, that is. That's what you hit, and you may hit a lob,
Or you may hit a drop shot, which falls flat against the wall —
"The wall?" you ask, and "Yes," I say, nor do I wish to stall,
But balls in this game bounce against not *just* one wall, but four,
And you climb in the box they make by ducking through a door.

"What kind of game is this?" you ask. "Who's heard of such a thing?"
And I reply that balls hit low will sometimes sort of ring
If they should hit the metal at the front wall's bottom part,
And then the game will stop before it once again will start.

If you have not yet guessed the name of this peculiar sport
Where balls are hit off walls and bounce around a little court,
A hint, perhaps, will help. Think of a vegetable, by gosh,
And then it will occur to you that I am talking *squash*.

POLO

There is this game called polo.
It's a splendid game, of course.
You swing a mallet at a ball
while riding on a horse.

You ride upon the horse, I mean.
The ball is on the ground,
And when you whack the ball,
it makes a very pleasing sound,

A kind of "thwock," I guess you'd say,
Much deeper than a "click,"
And doing all this on a horse
is quite a clever trick.

I'm sure the people playing polo
have a lot of fun.
The horses? I don't really know.
I've never questioned one.

NO POLE VAULTING FOR ME

There are some games that seem to me too dangerous to try,
And I would no more play them than I'd jump into the sky
If I were in an airplane and the door was open wide.
(Should anybody think I should, I'd run from them and hide.)

One game that I am thinking of is vaulting with a pole.
You run and jam this great long stick into a little hole,
And then you ride the stick into the air above the bar,
And, if you're lucky land where all the softest landings are
Within a pit that's like a bed of feathers or of foam,
And there you feel as safe as you could ever feel at home.

But what if, running with that pole, you miss a step or two?
The pole could end up anywhere, and so, perhaps, could you!
And what if, as you launch yourself and sail into the air,
You hear a dreadful cracking sound, and then the pole's not there?
Or maybe all the rest goes well until you start to glide
Up toward the bar you need to clear on your exciting ride,
When suddenly you lose your way and wobble just a bit,
And land on something cold and hard instead of in the pit?

So baseball? Sure, I'll play it, and at soccer I'll excel.
I'll swim against the fastest fish and volley balls as well.
But as for trying to clear the bar by vaulting with a pole,
I'll pass or punt, my friend, or somehow find a safer goal.

BOWLING

I think I've seen the future, and I think that it is bowling.
That is, I'm sure, the game toward which we'll all be shortly rolling.
For unlike football players, bowlers stay upon their feet.
They ply their trade indoors as well, and that cannot be beat.
(In summer there's conditioned air, in winter there is heat.)

Like baseball, bowling has its strikes, but where are baseball's spares?
They're players sitting on the bench about whom no one cares.
I guess that basketball's a game that's often worth the playing,
But if you are not very tall, is it for you? Just saying
That bowlers can be very tall, or bowlers can be short,
For height is no advantage when you're on the bowling court.
(That rhyme's okay. The sense is not, but now I'll try to rally,
For even I know bowling has no court; it has an alley.)

So will we all be bowling soon? Will other games be lost?
Perhaps about the time the tropics end up under frost,
But still it's fun to think about a crazy, distant day,
When bowling will be all that anybody wants to play.

RISKY GAMES

Monopoly played sloppily is not without a cost.
Green houses sliding off the board can easily be lost.
I guess, as well, a red hotel could also disappear
To hide in some dark corner for a week, a month, a year!

Those playing chess can make a mess if they have sticky fingers.
On peanut butter-coated pawns the sticky often lingers,
And bishops dipped in chocolate do not slide as once they did.
Of kings who've fallen into milk the kingdom should be rid.

Oh, in the yards of those with cards of each of the four suits,
You hear the birds that sing their words, and some of them are beauts!
But all the same, I've seen a game of cards played in the sun
Turn ugly in the wake of what those birds have sometimes done.

CHESS IN THE KITCHEN

Sometimes when you'd like to play,
The weather on that very day
Convinces you to stay inside,
Setting baseball dreams aside.
If teammates at the ball yard met,
You'd each and every one get wet.

On days like those, which are a mess,
You might consider learning chess,
A game that calls for lots of brains,
But one quite handy when it rains,
Because you and a friend are able
To play it at the kitchen table.
One good thing about that plan
Is that in kitchens people can
Find peanut butter, jelly, too,
And apples, cookies, milk, and you
And anyone who's playing chess,
Assuming you won't make a mess,
Can take a break from pawns and kings
And eat those very tasty things.

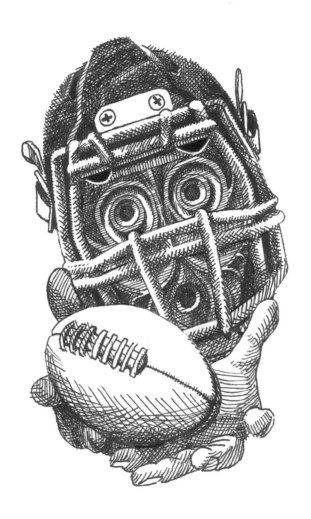

FOOTBALL FOR EVERYONE?

The boys were in the huddle.
That's where football players go.
And some of them were pretty fast, and some of them were slow,
And some of them were rather tall, and some of them were short,
But all of them were boys, of course, for that's who plays that sport —

Except that as they huddled up, an Amy wandered in —
An Amy — not an Abe or Al — and she said with a grin,
"I'd like to join your football game, so make some room for me."
The boys were mostly doubtful because they could plainly see
That though she wore a football shirt and wore a helmet, too,
She was a *she* and not a *he*, so what were they to do?

The question hung like fog above the football-playing bunch,
Until the spell was broken by a mother shouting, "Lunch!"
It was the mom of one small boy who lived across the street,
And when he heard his mother's voice, he ran right home to eat.
(For she had said she'd make him soup,
And chocolate milk as well,
And that beats football by a mile, as anyone can tell.)

This meant there was a spot, of course, the team was one boy short . . .
And down a player is no good, no matter what the sport,
So Amy joined the huddle, and although there were some grumbles,

When Amy got the ball, she did the job. There were no fumbles.
She caught a dozen passes, and she threw a couple, too,
And twice she ran for touchdowns, which the best of runners do,
And when the game was over and when Amy's team had won,
The boys agreed that playing with her had been kind of fun,
And one boy who was fond of winning asked her if she knew
Some other girls who'd like to play — and could she bring them too?

THE THANKSGIVING DAY GAME

It was just a mile's walk to the movie theater, where we'd all meet,
Having left our houses by nine because by two we would be eating
Our separate Thanksgiving turkeys, around our separate tables,
Our memories filled with visions of the big kids, muscles tight as cables,
As they'd performed their homecoming heroics for the town,
And for their old and famous coach, and for the cheers that they
        called down
From the wooden seats filled up with everyone we knew.
From behind the movie theater we followed the railroad track through
The woods, though we'd been told a hundred times not to,
And before we could see the field we could see the cold, blue
Sky over it, and hear the odd rumble of the old bass drum and people
        crowded together
At this crazy time of day in the morning, and hear the leather
Slap against the hands of the quarterbacks and the ends,
And one of us had a brother on the team, and so his friends
Could squeeze into the first row of seats along the home-team side.
But not for long. Restless, we'd climb the bleachers and slide
Along the railings and shout at each other and buy forbidden candy
Apples, and hot dogs, and peanuts, and orange soda — all dandy
Things to eat once a year in the morning at a game scheduled at ten
        for fear

That otherwise it would conflict with Thanksgiving, the biggest dinner
                    of the year.
And so we ran and crunched the cinders underneath our sneakers,
And raced on to the field at half time to test our weaker
Arms against those of the heroic players. The boys who had been us
Lounged against the rails along the stands, and watched the cheerleaders,
                    and cussed:
And the men who had been them asked their wives in scarves if they
                    were too cold,
And dug their hands into the pockets of their tweed sportscoats, and
                    felt the tug of being old
Enough to worry about whether they would have to leave early
If their wives were weary, or the baby cried, or the wind turned surly.
And then the game, which was the center of the day, would begin again,
And into the afternoon the biggest, strongest boy, who could be
                    comfortable with men,
Would take the ball and run past a boy who'd misread the play
And zigged when he should have zagged and would remember
                    Thanksgiving Day
Forever as the time he blew it, and allowed the winning touchdown.
And the hopeless, muffled band would play, and the cheerleaders
                    tumble around
The field in their wool sweaters, and grin and laugh at each other
Harder than any football game could account for. And the grandmothers
At home would look at the clock, and despair that the turkey would dry out,
But by then we would be back on the tracks, headed home, with no doubt

In our little minds that when we got there the bird would be brown and hot,
And the potatoes buttered and fluffy, and cranberry sauce, which was not
For any day other than Thanksgiving, like the morning football game
That brought the whole town out to shout up into the November sky
At what would be, or had been, and remember now with thanks in
the mind's eye.

SUPER BOWL

When I was small, and someone said "The Super Bowl," I thought
That it was some great dish that overflowed with stuff you bought!
With stuff like candy, surely, chocolate candy would be best,
But lollypops are good as well, and certainly the rest
Of that great dish, that Super Bowl, would never carry pickles.
Instead, between the chocolates, maybe there'd be dimes and nickels.

Unhappily, we all grow up, and I grew up as well,
And though I think the Super Bowl is sometimes kind of swell,
I still recall the Super Bowl about which I would dream —
And did I mention that it also featured peach ice cream?

I DO NOT LOVE THEE

I do not love thee, football game.
Your players limp away quite lame,
And every season it's the same.
I do not love thee, football game.

I do not love thee, referee.
You have two eyes but cannot see.
At least that's how it seems to me.
I do not love thee, referee.

I do not love thee, noisy crowd.
Your face is red. Your roar is loud.
Of someone else's deeds you're proud,
I do not love thee, noisy crowd.

I do not love thee, ticket price.
I'm eating only beans and rice
'cause you're so high. That's not so nice.
I do not love thee, ticket price.

I do not love thee, football game.
For that I can't say who's to blame —
But every season it's the same.
I do not love thee, football game.

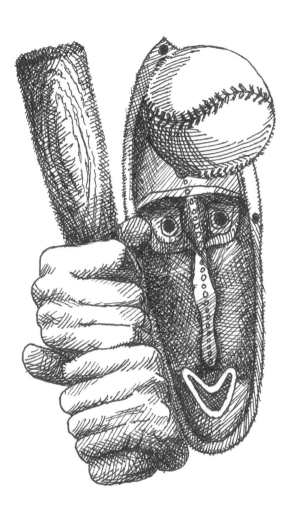

WILLIE MAYS

Willie Mays
Throughout his days
Of playing baseball well
Was celebrated far and wide,
And those who saw him tell
Of how the pitchers facing him
Would try to knock him down.
But Willie'd smile, shake his head,
And all about the town
The people who knew Willie, they would grin a little bit —
Beause they knew he'd get right up
And get himself a hit.

You didn't want to make him mad
If you were on the mound.
He'd dust himself off, smile, and then
He'd turn your pitch around,
Then trot around the bases
As it left the old ballpark,
And every Giants fan would cheer,
As happy as a lark.
Oh, he could hit, no doubt of that,
And he could run as well . . .

He'd leave his hat behind, sometimes,
And those who watched could tell
That any ball hit toward him, he could catch it on the fly —
One writer said his glove was where the triples went to die.
And once, against the Indians, in 1954,
He ran in centerfield until he couldn't anymore,
And stuck his glove into the air and caught the long fly ball
That no one but him could have caught, and that was not quite all . . .
He turned (and lost his cap, of course)
To make his mighty throw,
And all the runners on the bases had nowhere to go.
(For any Cleveland fan the telling of this story hurts.
The guy who hit the ball and saw it caught? That was Vic Wertz.)

But that was not the only day upon which Willie Mays
Made one of his amazing catches, his amazing plays.
He caught balls in Milwaukee, and in Brooklyn, and L.A.,
He caught them in the dead of night, and on each sunlit day,

When Willie hit a single, and only got to first,
Just when the pitchers looked toward home, he'd show a mighty burst
Of speed! Then, when they looked around, they'd see an empty space.
For Willie, who had been on first, would be on second base!

Was Willie Mays an all-star? He was almost always there.
He's also in the Hall of Fame, and should you ever care
To visit that museum full of hitters who were great,

And pitchers, fast or crafty, who threw sinkers that sunk late,
And managers who knew the tricks of winning baseball games,
And others so accomplished that you'd surely know their names
If I were to recite them — Hey, perhaps I'll try a few:
Babe Ruth, and Walter Johnson, and Cy Young, Clemente, too . . .
Ty Cobb, of course, and Sandy Koufax, also Satchel Paige,
Who pitched until he'd reached a ripish, oldish sort of age —
Well, Willie is among these guys, for he has earned his place,
And so the plaques in Cooperstown portray his well-known face.
His numbers are impressive, and they justify his fame,
But what was more impressive was the way he played the game.
He looked as if he couldn't wait to step up to the plate,
And even standing still, he somehow looked completely great.
And if you looked at baseball games for several million days,
You might not see a player quite as good as Willie Mays.

A SHORT POEM DEDICATED TO THE CELEBRATION OF AN AFTERNOON AND EARLY EVENING DURING WHICH THE MAJOR LEAGUE BASEBALL TEAM REPRESENTING THE CITIES OF ST. PAUL AND MINNEAPOLIS MANAGED TO SECURE TWO VICTORIES

Twins
Wins

OUT AT THE BALL GAME

Before you even reach the park, you hear the distant cheers.
You walk a little faster, and everybody nears
The entrance to the stadium, that looms above the street,
And ticket-sellers stand and wait, and you can smell the sweet
Aroma of the sausages that sizzle there beside
The old man selling peanuts, and the ice cream merchants ride
Their carts between the hungry people waiting to get in,
And kids and dads and moms all start to hope their team will win.

Once through the turnstiles, you can buy a pennant or a hat,
A program, or a jersey, or a little wooden bat,
A baseball signed by everyone who's on your favorite team,
A ball so special that you'd never in your wildest dream
Be using it for playing catch, or in a baseball game,
For stained with grass and dirt it couldn't ever be the same.
Then as you reach the tunnel that will take you to your seat,
You hear the music playing and you hear your folks repeat
The warning, "Stay beside me. Don't get lost among the crowd!"
But you can barely hear them, 'cause the ballpark is so loud.
And now you're in the stadium, and there, spread out below,
You see the greenest grass that any kid could ever know,
And on the grass the players, in their spotless baseball whites,
Are throwing baseballs back and forth, and all the lovely sights
That you have seen before this day seem pale beside the view
Of players warming up to do what you will see them do.

But first, before the game begins, you run down to the rail
Where someone's signing autographs, and there you do not fail
To get each favorite player's name, and each one smiles as well,
And then they turn back to their work, and anyone can tell
It's time for baseball to begin.

                                        The umpire shouts "Play ball!"
And you look toward the outfield and the distant, looming wall
And wonder, how can anybody hit the ball that far?
It seems a hundred miles from there to where the batters are.

But now the game is starting, and you settle in your seat.
You're looking for the popcorn seller when you hear the sweet
And solid sound of bat on ball. You look, and as you do,
The ball comes on a line from batter's box to almost you!
Then, luckily, it bounces off some clumsy guy in front,
And as he throws his hands up with a disappointed grunt,
The ball pops up into the air — you reach out and, oh boy!
You've got yourself a baseball and the day fills up with joy.

It doesn't always work that way. Sometimes, in fact, it rains,
And everybody drives back home and everyone complains,
And all the kids are cranky, the adults regret the plan
To travel to a baseball game. Still, anybody can
Construct a dream of going to a game that turns out well.
I hope when you next get to one, you'll have a tale to tell.

THE DISAPPEARING FAN

"Take me out to the ballgame!
Take me out with the crowd!
Buy me some peanuts and crackerjack!
I don't care if I never get back!"

(from "Take Me Out To The Ballgame")

For peanuts, even lots of them, and then some Crackerjack,
Would anybody cease to care if they did not get back?
The ballpark is a lovely place on any summer's day.
It's great to watch a game in which both teams have come to play,
But how long could a man survive upon that salty diet?
And would the ballpark still be fun when it was dark and quiet?
And when the gates were tightly locked and no one was around,
And traffic on the highway was the one and only sound
You heard as you were huddled in the bleachers all alone
With peanuts and with crackerjack, as 'round the winds did moan,
Would you not wish to get right back to some more comfy space,
Where you might find a glass of milk and some familiar face?

So take me to the ballgame, sure. I'd like to be included.
But if you think I'll stay forever, then you are deluded.
The crackerjack and peanuts notwithstanding, if I roam
To any ballgame, when it's over I'd as soon go home.

ANIMAL PLAYERS

If mice could pick up baseball bats
And wear those great big baseball hats
Could they be playing for the Cubs?
If not as starters, then as subs?

I wonder, too, if kangaroos,
If they were wearing baseball shoes,
Could help the Dodgers as they roam
And hop and bounce from third to home?

The Giants also might prevail
More often than they'd likely fail
If sometimes in the batter's box
They could employ a quick, brown fox.
(Don't say they shouldn't do it ever.
Foxes, I am told, are clever.)

The Pirates, when they make a switch
And need somebody else to pitch,
Might find a monkey to replace
A tired or unhappy ace.
But could a chimp be taught to throw
A ball where it would have to go

To lead the ump to shout out "Strike!
For that's a pitch that I quite like!"
I'd like to see in left a frog,
They rescued from a swampy bog.
With luck a stork might find a place
At first or third or second base,
While someone playing in right field
Could someday be convinced to yield
His spot to some four-legged pup
Who'd chase the ball and eat it up.

This is a harmless game I play
To get me through a rain delay.

BASEBALL CARDS

In Mom and Dad there's some concern
That maybe I will never learn
        Of math and science, great books, and the rest.
I do not think that they should worry.
What the heck, and what's the hurry?
        I am doing what I like the best.

Some, at my age, will learn to dance,
While others, given any chance,
        Are writing poems, seeking to be bards.
I guess I wish them all the best,
But I am different from the rest:
        I close my door and play with baseball cards.

I lay them out upon the floor,
Some set to field and some to score,
        And listen for the crowd's roar in my head.
Is this how I should spend the day
And half the night? Is this the way?
        Should I be doing something else instead?

I guess you might feel that I should.
Perhaps I'm doing no one good
       As I sit with my baseball cards and dream.
But maybe you will change your mind
When you look up one day to find
       There's been a payoff to my goofy scheme.
For when I'm grown, I'll find the guy
Who owns the Sox or Yanks, and I
       Will manage, for him, his real baseball team.

MOM, I'M GOING TO BE A STAR

"Mom, I'm going to be a star."

"I love you, child, for what you are."

"But I will make a million dollars,
Generating hoots and hollers!
All the fans will shout my name!"

"Maybe, child, and all the same,
I will love you all my days,
If you do or don't win praise."

"Mom, I'll build a house for you,
And it will have an ocean view."

"That, my child, would be quite grand.
Now sit with me and hold my hand,
And know, in case you don't succeed,
It's time for you to learn to read."

SEVEN-YEAR OLD SOCCER PLAYER

The player dreams of double-dips.
Her father dreams of scholarships.
(The scoop of chocolate's on the top . . .
She hopes it won't half melt and drop.)

Her father hopes she'll play until
She dents the big tuition bill
With shots that leave the keeper weeping.
These are dreams he has while sleeping.

She has fun among her friends,
Knowing, if that ever ends,
That some new game will find its way
Into the time she has for play.

If that happens, he will smile,
Sadly, maybe, for a while,
But he is not the sort of dad
Who'd ever let that make him mad.

KICKING A ROCK

There's much to be said for kicking a rock.
You don't need an umpire. You don't need a clock.
It works on the street or the grass or a dock.
There's much to be said for kicking a rock.

And maybe on days when you're off on your own,
You ought to consider just kicking a stone,
For whether you're small or entirely grown,
There's much satisfaction in kicking a stone.

I don't mean a boulder. A boulder won't do.
And you shouldn't kick anything without your shoe,
But if you're inclined, then a thing you might do
Is you might kick a rock or a stone, that is true.

You can kick it and measure how far it can go,
Kick it over a curb or a small pile of snow,
And then you announce in a voice proud but low
That your rock set a record, though no one will know.

A SHORT REFUTATION OF THE ANCIENT WISDOM THAT PARENTS HAVE PASSED ALONG TO THOSE OF THEIR CHILDREN WHOM THEY CAUGHT PLAYING A GAME THAT REQUIRED COMPETITORS TO USE VARIOUS PARTS OF THEIR BODIES TO CAUSE A JACKKNIFE TO STICK INTO THE GROUND

Though I have played at mumblety-peg,
I do not lack an arm or a leg.
I have two eyes, and look at those:
I've got ten fingers and ten toes.

MARBLES AND BARBELLS

If you had to choose between marbles and barbells
Would you even know where to start?
See, marbles are light, and the barbells are heavy,
And that's just the easiest part.

With marbles you play on the ground in the sun.
With barbells you wouldn't have nearly the fun
That you have shooting marbles with friends in the dirt —
And with barbells it's more likely that you'll get hurt.
You'll understand this when I say, I suppose
That a barbell would hurt if it fell on your toes,
While a marble, dropped carelessly, wouldn't hurt much.
Would you even notice its marble-y touch?

Of course, lifting barbells might make muscles grow,
And muscles are useful wherever you go.
They'd grow in your arms and your legs and your back —
And help you lift marbles that came in a sack.

POGO STICKING

"This dream of flying," my dad said. "It's completely IN-sane.
Unless you get on the laptop there, and buy yourself a ticket on an AIR-plane.
In which case you can go to San Antonio, or Madrid, or even Zanzibar,
Although if you asked me if I'd ever gone there, I'd have to acknowledge that
I never did.
Or at least not Zanzibar."

But the crazy dream wouldn't go away. I had it every night. And it was ter-IFF-ic,
Although you'd be out of luck if you asked me to be any more spe-CIF-ic.
But I knew I was flying, looking down on trees and houses and dogs yapping
up at me,
Because if you're not flying, that's not the sort of thing you're ever gonna see,
So there I was, above the roof tops over which Santa Claus sails on Christmas
Eve in his sled,
Or at least that's what he does on behalf of children who have behaved
themselves, according to what lots of people have said,
Perhaps even in Zanzibar.

And the soaring and sailing and looking down at everything from heavy
traffic on the highway to fields of growing grass
Would have *just* been a dream, I suppose, and perhaps it would have been
destined to utterly pass,
Just as lots of things that children dream about never end up being anything
other than dreams,

Or at least once those children get older and supposedly wiser, that's
                    pretty much the way it seems,
Except that one night my dad, who'd said flying was insane, came home
                    with a pogo stick,
And before long I'd mastered the thing, which is not such an easy trick,
Whether on the sidewalk in front of your home
                    or in Zanzibar.

But I didn't just bounce in the driveway, or up and down on the sidewalk,
                    or even on the school basketball court,
Though I guess for most kids that would have been enough pogo-sticking,
                    and then they'd have moved on to some other sport.
                    Whether or not they'd been in Zanzibar.
But not me.
I yearned to be free.
I wanted to look down on the tops of all the things the tops of which I
                    had never been able to see.
So I pogo'ed and pogo'ed, and pogo'ed some more,
Until what had been the ceiling began to seem like it might one day be
                    the floor,
And I bounced up so high that I might just as *well* have been flying,
And I did it for so long that it felt like I could do it without half trying . . .
                    Though I never did reach Zanzibar.

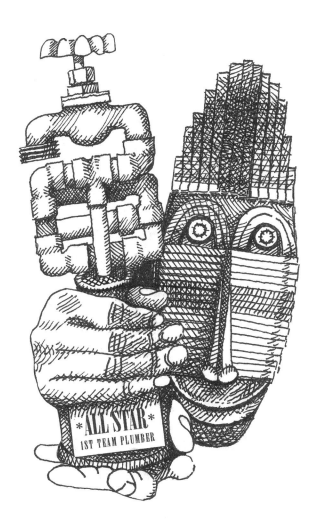

ALL STARS

There should be all-star architects, and all-star plumbers, too.
The latter could all gather to clear pipes clogged up with goo,
While thousands cheer the water whooshing down the pristine drains.
There should be all-star astronauts; and researchers with brains
More active than the brains of those who work in other labs
Should also be named all-stars, even if their pecs and abs
Don't bulge. All-star mechanics should be honored for their touch
With cranky engines, and for never charging us so much
That we must dig into our savings to reclaim our cars.
There should be all-star waiters, too, and folks who work in bars
Should also be called all-stars if they're pleasant and discreet —
And shouldn't maids be all-stars if the rooms they clean are neat?
There should be all-star singers, those who never miss a note,
And sing with spontaneity, and not as if by rote.
And all-star painters wouldn't paint themselves into a rut;
They'd never spatter paint around or paint the windows shut.
When I'm in a convenience store, and I'm served by a jerk
Who's stoned or lost in space, I wish I had an all-star clerk —
A man or woman, boy or girl, who doesn't snarl or bite,
And can provide directions if I'm lost alone, at night,
And not just shrug and tell me that he doesn't know the way
To any place I'm going *so just hurry up and pay.*
There should be all-star help-desk folks, who, though they know it all,
Don't make the rest of us feel dumb each time we have to call.

There should be all-star cleaners, who would never lose our stuff,
And all-star blackjack dealers saying, *Pal, you've lost enough,*
And point us toward the door before we pawned our shirt and shoes.

The all-star games for athletes always make the TV news,
But why should they have all the fun, and all the glory, too?
There should be all-star everythings. No matter what you do,
You should be on the ballot, though I don't know who would vote.
And, as an all-star — when you won — I'm sure you wouldn't gloat.

WHY IT'S EASIER TO BE A SPORTSWRITER THAN AN ATHLETE

In basketball, you should be tall.
A jockey should be short.
A tennis player should be quick
To get around the court.

A runner must be fast, of course,
A pole-vaulter must bend.
But those who write about our sports?
Well, let me tell you, friend,

They can be tall or short, I guess,
And limp or lose their hair
And all their clothes can be a mess . . .
For writers needn't care,

How well they hit or throw or field.
They keep their jobs through time,
For aging writers needn't yield.
(At least if they can rhyme.)

acknowledgments

Thanks to Jim Kates for his sense of humor and for coming up with the title.

Thanks to Cris Mattison for the design of the book, and thanks to old friend Steve Coren for his marvelous drawings.

Thanks to our daughters, Amy and Alison, for the joy they've given us, and most importantly thanks and love to my wife, Mary. From the first time I mentioned the idea to her, she was certain the book would be fun and told me so.

index

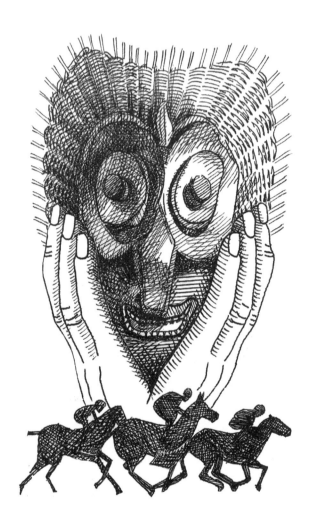